Tree of Life

Celtic Prayers to
the Universal Christ

ANAMCHARA BOOKS
Vestal, New York 13850
www.AnamcharaBooks.com

These are original prayers, written in the "Celtic style" by the author. Many of them are inspired by more ancient prayers, including those found in the *Carmina Gadelica*.

IngramSpark 2020 paperback ISBN:
978-1-62524-800-8

Cover design by Ellyn Sanna.
Interior design by Micaela Grace.

Tree of Life

Celtic Prayers to the Universal Christ

RAY SIMPSON

O Christ, the Tree of Life,
the blossoms on
the branches are your people.
The singing birds are your angels;
the whispering breeze is your Spirit.
O Christ, the Tree of Life,
may the blossoms bring forth
the sweetest fruit.
May the birds sing out
the highest praise;
may your Spirit cover all
with her gentle breath.

Contents

Introduction

Christians believe that Jesus of Nazareth was God incarnated in a human body; he was a historical person who walked this earth some two thousand years ago. We often use the words "Jesus" and "Christ" interchangeably for this person. Or we think of these words the way we might think of "Tom Jones" or "Sally Smith"—but "Jesus" is not the first name of the incarnated God, and "Christ" is not his last name. "Christ" was not his name but his title, defining his role. The name is the Greek translation of "Messiah," and it means "Anointed One."

Theologians in the twentieth and twenty-first centuries have recovered a very ancient understanding of the meaning of Christ. "What if Christ is a name for the immense spaciousness of all true Love?" That is the question Richard Rohr asks in his book *The Universal Christ*. He goes on to ask: "What if Christ refers to an infinite horizon that pulls us both from within and pulls us forward, too? What if Christ is another name for every thing—in its fullness?"

This concept of Christ points to a Being who is deeper, wider, and older than either Jesus of Nazareth or the Christian religion. "In the beginning was the Word," says the Gospel of John. The full expression of God, Divine revelation through the physical world—the Word—existed from the very beginning of Creation. The human being named Jesus is the Incarnation of that.

Franciscan theologian Zachary Hayes writes that the universe happens when God's Word comes pouring into nothingness. This means, say Hayes, that if the universe is the external embodiment of the Divine Word, "there is something Incarnational throughout the whole of creation." Like a vast, ever-growing Tree of Life, Christ—the expression of Divine love—expands endlessly throughout the universe.

This is a perspective that Celtic Christianity has always held. For the earliest Celtic saints, Nature was the "first book of God"; it was the Word, the Divine revelation expressed in forms we can see and touch. John Scotus Eriugena, the ninth-century Celtic theologian, taught that Creation is the direct expression of Divine love.

Duns Scotus, another medieval Celtic theologian, believed that from the very beginning God intended to enter Creation through the Incarnation of Christ in Jesus. He rejected the idea that the Incarnation was God's response to human sin. The reason for Christ's Incarnation in Jesus, Duns Scotus said, was not sin but the fullness of God's love. Through the specificity of the Incarnation—the Christ revealed in a particular, historical human being—all of us, and in fact all of Creation, is also invited to participate more fully in Divine love. In doing this, we too become "Christs," and we come into our fullest, most complete identities.

Celtic Christianity focuses on the individual; we are each capable of our own unique relationship with the Divine, without the need to rely on any organized religious institution. This is the process of becoming "Christ-like." Duns Scotus expressed this concept through a principle he referred to as *haecceitas*, which means, literally, "this-ness." Each of us is a one-of-a-kind expression of the Divine.

This idea is rooted in the understanding that because Christ is expressed in each detail of Creation, each thing inherently possesses its own dignity and goodness. Each thing, from paramecium to human beings, from subatomic particles to the whirling stars, reveals God uniquely, simply by being what it is.

Each thing is sacred, for everything is a word of God.

This is the perspective that Ray Simpson reveals in his poem-prayers. Inspired by traditional Celtic prayers, he gives word to our individual relationships with God and calls us to grow into Christ through our own "this-ness." His words speak of the wonder and beauty and love that God reveals to us through Christ, the Tree of Life that includes all that is.

"Christ is the visible image of the invisible God," says Colossians 1. "He existed before anything was created and is supreme over all creation, for through him God created everything in the heavenly realms and on earth. He made the things we can see and the things we can't see—such as thrones, kingdoms, rulers, and authorities in the unseen world. Everything was created through him and for him. He existed before anything else, and he holds all creation together. . . . For God in all his fullness was pleased to live in Christ (15–17, 19 NLT).

And, as Franciscan theologian Ilia Delio says, "Each of us is a little word of the Word of God, a mini-incarnation of divine love." This is both comfort and challenge. Delio goes on to say:

> The journey inward requires surrender to this mystery in our lives and this means letting go of our control buttons. It means dying to the untethered selves that occupy us daily; it means embracing the sufferings of our lives, from the little sufferings to the big ones, it means allowing God's grace to heal us, hold us and empower us for life. It means entering into darkness, the unknowns of our lives, and learning to trust the darkness, for the tenderness of divine love is already there.

May Ray's prayers help us do all that, so that each of us may more deeply participate in the Divine nature (1 Peter 1:4). May we each take our place in the Tree of Life, growing into our full potential as God's words to our world.

—Ellyn Sanna

Anamchara Books

One

Prayers
of Worship

May Christ rise in glory,
scattering the darkness.
The Sun of suns,
the eye of the great God,
the eye of the King of hosts,
is rising upon us,
gently and generously.
Welcome, glorious Son,
dawn of a new day.

Your glory, O Christ, be seen
in work that is done from the heart.
Your glory be seen
in work that meets true needs.
Your glory be seen in communication
that ennobles the spirit.
Your glory, O Christ, be seen
in beauty of form and friendship.

For the glory of creation
streaming from your heart
we praise you.
For the air of the eternal
seeping through the physical
we praise you.
For the everlasting glory
dipping into time
we praise you.
For the wonder of your presence
beckoning from each leaf
we praise you.
For setting us,
like the stars in their courses,
within the orbit of your love
we praise you.

Lord of the Dance, grant me joy in all things
in the towel that rubs my body,
the steam that heats my coffee,
the street that greets my feet
and the wonder of a life.

Unto you, O Christ, be praise for
every flower that ever grew,
every bird that ever flew,
every wind that ever blew.

Unto you, O Christ, be praise for
every flake of virgin snow,
every place where humans go,
every joy and every woe.

Unto you, O Christ, be praise for
every life that shall be born,
every heart that shall be torn.
every day and every dawn.

Thank you for
the taste of good food,
the crying of the wind
and the pulsing of our bodies.

Thank you for the cartwheels of the heart
the playing of a child
and the diving of a fish.

Power of powers, we worship you.
Light of lights, we worship you.
Life of lives, we worship you.

Source of life, we turn to you.
Savior of life, we turn to you.
Sustainer of life, we turn to you.

Love before time, we adore you.
Love in darkest time, we adore you.
Love in this time, we adore you.

Maker of all creatures, we honor you.
Friend of all creatures, we honor you.
Force of all creatures, we honor you.

You are the Food
from which all souls are fed.
You who gave birth to the universe
are born again in us.
Alleluia!

Christ, you are the glory of eternity
shining now among us,
the tenderness of God here with us now.
God who is with us, we adore you.
Christ, you are the Healing Person,
the pattern of goodness,
the fulfilment of the highest human hopes.
God who is with us, we adore you.

Christ, you are the champion of the weak,
the counsellor of the despairing,
the Lover of us all.
God who is with us, we adore you.
Christ, you are the splendor of the Creator,
our Bridge between heaven and earth.
God who is with us, we adore you.

Christ, you are the Source of life,
the Goal of the universe,
the people's Friend, the world-pervading God.
God who is with us, we adore you.

Christ, you are one of the human family,
Joy of Angels, Prince of Peace.
God who is with us, we adore you.

We give you worship with our whole life.
We give you praise with our whole tongue.
We give you service with our whole body.
We give you love with our whole heart.
We give you honor with our whole desire.
We give you our best thought,
our deeds, our words,
our will, our understanding,
our relationships,
our intellect, our journey, our end.

We love you, Christ, and we lift our voices
to honor you and to rejoice.
As thirsty deer go down to the pool,
so our thirsty souls are refreshed in you.
By day you guide us along the way;
at night you guard and with us stay.

Two

Prayers for Guidance on Life's Journey

Guide us, our great Mentor,
through the ups and downs of life.
Strengthen us to leave behind
what hinders our calling,
and to keep moving
toward ever-greater reality.

Help us, Great Christ-Spirit,
to live in you as fish live in water,
soar with you as birds fly in air,
run for you as deer run in woods,
flow with you as water flows in streams,
blaze for you as twigs burn in fire.

Day by day, dear Christ:
teach us from your word and your world;
lead us on our pilgrimage of life;
help us to live in your rhythms;
spur us to overcoming prayer;
strip from us all that clutters;
cherish through us your creation;
heal through us what is broken;
blow us to places beyond our comfort zones;
inspire us to foster unity;
reach out through us
with your justice, truth, and love,
that we may be aflame
and struggle for you forever.

O Being of truth,
O Being of sight,
O Being of wisdom,
give us judgment in our choices.

O Being of life,
O Being of peace,
O Being of time,
be with us now.

We quieten our souls
under the stillness of sky.
Peace be upon our breath.
Peace be upon our eyes.
Peace be upon our hearts.

Open our eyes to your presence.
Open our eyes to your call.
Open our hearts to your mercies,
that you may be all in all.

Forgive our sins of omission:
our pride and our thoughtless ways;
forgive our sins of commission:
the tongues that lead others astray.

Take from us sloth and apathy,
all spirit of blame or despair.
Give us eyes for fresh ventures,
that we may sweep through the air.

Great Spirit,
help us to relax into your plan for us.
Unfold it for us
as the acorn unfolds into the oak.

Kindle our imaginations.
Rivet our attention with graphic truth.
Restock our memories with noble themes.

Make us eager to align our wills with yours.
Give us joy in our hearts, keep us serving.
May we grow in intimacy with you
until each one of our acts
is a glad response to your promptings.

Christ, with joy we pledge our love of you.
We are no longer our own but yours.
Put us to what you will,
place us with whom you will;
let us be put to work for you
or put aside for you;
let us be full, let us be empty;
let us have all things, let us have nothing.

We freely and, with all our heart,
give you all things for you to use.
May we walk together with you
into the community that nothing can destroy.

Give me the ambition
to use everything I have
for the highest purposes;
to abuse no person,
to misuse no powers,
to harness skills to service,
and to bring great things to flower.

Christ, may these graces flower
as never before:
the grace of authenticity and trust,
the grace of forgiving love and laughter,
the maturity of pity
for those who manipulate.

Help me to be true to myself and true to you.
Help me to be true to others
and true to the call.
Help me to be true to earth
and true to heaven.

Lead us from that
which binds to that which frees;
lead us from that
which cramps to that which creates;
lead us from that
which lies to that which speaks truth;
lead us from that
which blights to that which ennobles;
lead us from that
which hides to that which celebrates;
lead us from that
which fades to that which endures.

Lead us from showing off to showing love;
lead us from being unreal to being real;
lead us from that which is partial
to that which makes whole.

Lead us from that which is false
to that which is real;
lead us from that which is self-centered
to that which is good;
lead us from that which fades
to that which endures.

Mighty Anchor in our storms,
brightest Light in our darkness,
lead us from despair to hope,
contempt to praise
falsehood to truth,
hatred to love,
violence to peace.

Spirit of Christ, be wild and free in us.
Batter our proud and stubborn wills.
Blow us where you choose.
Break us down if you must.
Refashion us as you will.
Move us powerfully away
from the games we play to try to tame you.

Lead us into the wild places,
the places of dreams or screams,
the long dark tunnels
or the wide, sunny vistas.
Teach us to speak to lions,
to move mountains,
to bear tragedy,
and to mirror you.

Give us your firelight, Holy Christ-Spirit,
as we go down
into the things stored in our memories,
dreams and hurts.
Journey with us beyond these
to the seed of our nature you planted in us
at our beginning.
May we become that seed,
which is our true Self,
and may it grow and produce much fruit.

Divine Artist,
you uniquely shape our characters,
endow us with gifts
and pattern our lives.
May your inspired fingers work upon us,
that we may become your work of art.

Source of Creativity,
teach us to dance with the playful clouds
and to laugh with the glinting sun.

Teach us
to flow like the sparkling streams
and to soar like the high-winged birds.

Teach us
to dream of rainbow and mountains,
and to attempt to make our dreams real.

Teach us
to restock memory's treasure-house
and to give it all away.

Heroic Love,
help us in our vulnerability
not to retreat, close up, or pretend,
but to think clearly, act decisively,
confront lovingly,
and go wherever you send.

Christ of the gentle heart,
we place ourselves under your yoke.
We plan our diaries by your priorities.
We direct our feet along your way.
Help us to
see clearly,
act courageously,
and move on calmly
day by day.

Remove the clutter from our lives, O Christ,
and give us the grace of blessed simplicity.
Remove the divided affections from our lives,
O Christ,
and give us the grace of undivided love for all.
Remove the dominating spirit from our lives,
O Christ,
and give us the grace of seeking the good
in the other.

Help us to live simply
that others may simply live.
Free us from false attachments,
that we may be
true to ourselves,
true to others,
and true to you.

Impart to us imagination
to find the places in people
where we may connect.
Give us the grace of self-acceptance,
that we may accept a gift from another.
Grace us with love that empowers us
to share of ourselves.

Break the ties that bind us to our past;
free us to go wherever you direct.
Bless the tiredness
that blinds us to your presence;
grace us with
the scents of the company of heaven.
Burden us with the evils
that would ravage your children;
spur us to struggle until the tide is turned.

Teach us to leave behind
the things that tie our spirits down
and learn again to be your pilgrim people:
through fasting from
the frenzied feeding of false desires,
through study of your word,
meditation, and acts of service
restore the clearness of our seeing
and free us to share your generous love
with all.

You who are Heroic Love,
alive in every leaf and lane,
beckon us through star and stone
to stride across our petty ways
in pursuit of the Endless Adventure.

Christ, you know each of us by name,
more intimately than anyone else.
Help us to notice,
from among the countless thoughts
that cross our minds,
the thoughts that come as a gift
from Someone who knows us from the inside.
In other words,
help us to recognize your Voice.

Word of God,
out of the silence of eternity
you ceaselessly speak to your children.
Teach us to listen,
not to the discordant babble of a sick society,
but to the treasures of truth
in the deeps of silence.

Stretch our hearts, Christ,
and broaden our minds.
Open our eyes, Christ,
that we may find:
fresh horizons,
a holy grail,
a noble challenge,
a height to scale,
and the theme of our sleep.
Be the shape in the gloom
and the piercing of darkness.
All-seeing One,
may our vision be yours.

You whose heroic love
comes in a thousand ways:
May we be the clay
that laughs in the hands of the potter,
sails borne by the wind,
trees earthed in the soil,
dancers in tune with the rhythm.

Show us, Christ,
that for which the time has come,
be it small or great.
Show us what lies in this moment.
Show us what you are bringing to a head,
or bringing to an end, or bringing to birth.
And we will obey.

Speak, Christ,
in stillness or storm,
in circumstance or sign,
in Scripture or word,
in conscience or heart,
in encounter or art.
Stir up the gift in us.

Christ, our Vision,
impelled by the visions you entrust to us,
may we break through
the brittle shell of our unbelief
and move, untrammeled,
toward the heavenly horizons.

Universal Christ, you have a plan
for every person
and for every situation in the world.
But we are so dim.
We are so deaf.
Help us to become
Christ-guided instruments
and always be in just the place
you wish us to be.

Thank you, Christ,
that even if
we are difficult or blinkered people,
you can put holy desires into our hearts
and divine intimations before our eyes
so that we come through obstacles
to our eternal resurrection.

Christ, grant me the strength
to do without things.
Grant me the wisdom
to see the "within" of things.
Grant me the knowledge
to take the measure of evil spirits.
Grant me understanding
to know you who alone are true.

Infinite One of the wise heart,
Saving One of the clear sight,
Knowing One of the hidden deeps,
may I learn from you as an eager pupil.
May I learn from life as a humble child.
May I learn from night, may I learn from day.
May I learn from soul friends,
may I learn from stillness.

Christ, you remember us
and know our every thought.
Help us to remember you,
and know your words to us.

Make us attentive to your clear commands.
Make us attentive
to the sighing of your world.
Make us attentive to your whispering tones.
Make us attentive to your slightest wish.

Eternal Truth,
grant us humility to know how little we know.
Give us clarity to know
what is best for us to learn.
Show us a good way to this.
Form us in the art of asking useful questions.
Help us grow, like Jesus, in understanding.

Holy True and Real One.
Help us to be true, help us to be real.
Help us to know our own mind.
Help us to know what we must say yes to
and what we must say no to.
May our lives be like a blank sheet of paper,
ready for you to write your words.

Help us to know and accept our limits.
Help us to mind the gaps—
to honor you by keeping margins,
to receive as well as to give,
to be a sign of renewal,
for Christ's sake.

Open our eyes to the poisons of our time,
　　that we may avoid them.
Alert us to the angry horses of our time,
　　that we may calm them.
Prepare us for the prowling lions of our time,
　　that we may bring them to nothing.

Divine Source of Truth,
Beauty, and Goodness,
our minds are like a field.
In this field, please grow many good things,
many beautiful things,
and many true things with deep roots.
Teach us also how to weed and sift and sort,
how to water and prune wisely.

We pray for the cleansing of our perceptions,
that we may hear,
that we may see,
that we may understand with our hearts
and that we may be healed.

Help us to breathe in step with you.
Help us to know the time.
Help us to go with the flow.

Teach us, dear Christ, to
know your ways,
explore your world,
learn from mistakes,
understand people,
manage time and talents,
weave meaning out of memory,
gain insight from inspired people,
grow into the stature of Christ.

Christ, unlock the treasures of wisdom to us,
but first give us hearts for humble learning.

Train us
to trade with the gifts you have granted us,
to teach with the knowledge
you have grown in us,
to touch the lives you have given us.

Forgetting what is past,
we look to the things unseen.
We journey in your light.

The sun shall not strike us by day,
nor the moon by night.
We journey in your light.

We look not to right or left,
but straight toward your way.
We journey in your light.

The rough places shall be smoothed
and the pitfalls shall be cleared.
We journey in your light.

The proud shall be brought low
and the humble shall be raised up.
We journey in your light.

The hungry shall be fed
and the poor shall have good news.
We journey in your light.

No final home have we
on this life's passing seas.
High King of land and sea,
wherever we go is yours.
We journey in your light.

Incomparable Guide,
Help us to travel light
and so to know joys of discovery.
Help us to shed prejudice,
and so to be strangers no longer
but pilgrims together.
Help us to stop trying to control,
and so to let things happen
and to find you in the journeying.

Call, call, call, great Chief of the high hills.
Call, call, call, great Christ of the far paths.
Call, call, call, great Counsellor
of the near gate.
Set our spirits free to soar wherever you climb.
Set our feet free to trek wherever you go.
Set our mouths free
to say whatever you command.

May the Christ who walks with wounded feet
walk with us on the road.
May the Christ who serves
with wounded hands
stretch out our hands to serve.
May the Christ who loves
with the wounded heart
open our hearts to love.

Christ, be within us to give us strength,
over us to protect us,
beneath us to support us,
in front of us to be our guide,
behind us to prevent us falling away,
surrounding us to give us courage;
so that alone, alone
we may walk into the great unknown.

You who are Heroic Love
have built adventure into each day
and into every life.
Help us to explore, to overcome,
and to step out toward this day's horizons
in the spirit of Christ,
the Endless Adventurer.

Each day we travel through this life
may we sense you in the taste of good food,
in the crying of the wind
and in the messages of our bodies.
May we see you in the wild flower
or the playing of a child.
May we know you in the sap of our bodies
or embrace you in their disintegration,
but always travel with you.

O Christ, we thank you
that you have called us to travel,
no longer as strangers,
but as pilgrims together
on the journey of your people on earth.
Lead us in the paths
that are life-giving for the world.

Sweet All-Aware One,
Grant me the grace to find the place
where you alone suffice;
where you are in the soil on which I sit,
and stand and lay my head
there on your face to gaze.

Forgive us for
grasping at things we do not need,
clinging to projects that distract us from you,
accumulating worries
that hold us back from your path.
Help us to acquire what no money can buy:
a free spirit,
a wise mind,
a beautiful attitude,
a serving heart.

Boundless Nourisher,
help me to retreat in order to advance;
to reorientate my life with you.
Help me to relax and listen,
to observe and receive;
perhaps to walk in the steps of saints,
or to read and reflect and renew my mind.
Above all may I stop running away,
and learn to wonder as I wander with you.

I will come apart from life with you,
Lord Christ,
that you may still my heart.
I will come apart from the world with you,
Lord Christ,
that you may restock my mind.
I will come apart from all the distracts me
from you, Lord Christ,
that you may steel my will.
I will retreat with you, Lord Christ,
that together we may advance.

Lead, me, Christ, into a place of prayer
to live simply, silently, and alone with you
so that I may die to myself quicker
and you may grow in me faster;
so that you may give more of yourself
to the world that hungers for you.

Life of Christ, Sun of suns,
filling every part of us,
life be in our speech,
sense in what we say.
Love be in our deeds
till you come back again.

Love of Christ, Sun of suns,
filling every heart for us,
love be in our deeds,
thought be in our words.
Care be in our mien
till you come back again.

Christ, Pattern of Goodness,
be our Pattern today.
Christ, Hope of the weak,
be our Hope today.
Christ, Fulfiller of our longings,
be our Fulfiller today.
Christ, Bridge between earth and heaven,
be our Bridge today.

Christ, give us that love
that does not fail people;
make our lives like an open fire
that you are always kindling,
which nothing can quench.

O Christ most sweet,
may we receive perpetual light from you,
so that the world's darkness
may be driven from us.
O eternal Priest, may we see you,
observe you, desire you, and love you alone
as you shine in your eternal temple.

Eternal Light, shine into our hearts.
Eternal Goodness, deliver us from evil.
Eternal Power, strengthen us.
Eternal Wisdom,
scatter the darkness of our ignorance.
Eternal Pity, have mercy on us.
With our whole being we shall seek your face
until we are brought to your holy presence.

Christ be within us,
Christ be beside us,
Christ in the stranger,
Christ in the friend,
Christ in our speaking,
Christ in our thinking,
Christ in our working,
Christ at our end.

Teach us, dear Christ,
to be lifelong disciples;
to think your thoughts after you,
to develop a sense of wonder,
to trace your hand in history,
to understand the times;
to distinguish the true from the false,
to relate the part to the whole,
to see and serve the greatness in others.

Christ with us;
be in my waking and working
be in my cleaning and counting.

Christ with us;
be in my talking and texting
be in my shopping and sharing.

Christ in the little things:
Christ in this thing;
Christ in that thing;
Christ in all things.

Christ of the Journey,
you allowed yourself to travel alone
when necessary,
but you invited treasured friends
to share much of the journey with you:
sacred moments and frightening ordeals;
humdrum tasks, tiring days, draining duties.
Share our journey.
Bring us to companions on the way
who are true friends of our souls.

Make us pilgrims of the world
until we see your face in everyone we meet.
Make us pilgrims of the grail
until we see your grace
in every place we visit.
Make us pilgrims of the road
until we see your prints in every chore we do.

Three

Prayers for Others

Christ, Mediator between earth and heaven,
through you we share with these our love.
We entrust them to you
because you alone are trustworthy
and your compassion knows no end.

Divine Upbringer
who calls each of your children by name,
we remember with gratitude
your many faithful servants
who, though they are neither known to us
nor great in this world's eyes,
are like precious jewels to you.

Bless, Sacred One, those who
shine in the world and light up our way,
bring faith to birth as spiritual midwives,
accept death rather than deny God,
seek the dignity of life and labor,
foster appreciation of diverse cultures,
shepherd their people in sincerity of heart,
say yes to your callings.

(At Death)

Since it was you, O Christ,
who bought each soul—
at the time it gave up its life,
at the time of severing the breath,
at the time of returning to dust
at the time you delivered judgement—
may your peace be
on your ingathering of souls.
Christ, Body of God,
your peace be upon your own ingathering.

Christ forsaken,
have mercy on all who are forsaken.
Christ afraid,
have mercy on all who are afraid.
Christ betrayed,
have mercy on all who are betrayed.
Christ unnoticed,
have mercy on all who are unnoticed.

Healing power of Christ,
penetrate the brittle shell
of the ones for whom we pray.
Where they are no longer present to others,
attract them to your gaze.
Where they are down and out,
grasp hold of them and raise them up.
Where they are fettered,
set them free to leap and praise.

The Divine Gift come into your loss.
The Divine Peace come into your dread.
The Divine Hope come into your despair.
The Divine Helper come to your aid.

Into your loss,
come,
O Being of Gift,
O Being of Peace,
O Being of Life eternal.

Into your threat,
come,
O Being of Strength,
O Being of Peace,
O Being of Life eternal.

Into your despair,
come,
O Being of Hope,
O Being of Peace,
O Being of life eternal.

Into your devastation,
come,
O Being of Love,
O Being of Peace,
O Being of life eternal.

The blessing of acceptance be yours.
The blessing of forgiveness be yours.
The blessing of gentleness be yours.
The blessing of resilience be yours.
The blessing of eternal life be yours.

When a person sails by with eyes all glazed,
may our eyes give them rays of love.
When a person passes, cold or hard,
may our hearts melt them
with welcoming warmth.

Bring to flower in your children
the seeds that dormant lie.
In those who have none to encourage them,
bring the seeds of confidence to flower.
In those who are trapped
by their circumstances,
bring the seeds of possibility to flower.
In those who find it difficult to learn,
bring the seeds of understanding to flower.
In those at the bottom of the social pile,
bring the seeds of empowerment to flower.

Four

Prayers for Healing and Wholeness

Free me, Immense Spirit,
from a lifetime's crippling habits,
from a closed and cabined mind,
from a cowering, timid spirit,
from blinkered, haughty habits,
to be who I am, clothed and in my right mind.

We are appealing to you,
since you are the Ruler of Heaven.
We are praying to you,
since you are the Sovereign of Good.
Lift each wasting,
each weariness and sickness.
Lift each soreness and discomfort,
We are keenly praying to you.
Lift each stiffness
as you separate earth from ocean.

Thrice-seeing King of Heaven,
dislodge the mote that is in my blind eye
and gently place it on my tongue
where I can spit it out.

Life-giver, Pain-bearer, Being of Love,
you hold in your heart our names
and the hurts we cannot bear to speak of.
You journey with us through pain
until you reconcile
all that we have rejected in ourselves
and no part of your creation is alien to us.

Help us, O Healing One,
to stop dwelling
on what others achieve that we don't.
As we look on the pattern
in the palm of each hand,
we thank you that each is uniquely personal.
May we grow in confidence,
love, and creativity
according to the designs you have for us.
We forgive the ones who make us feel inferior.
Meet their needs;
help them find their best course.
Heal and have mercy on us all.

As nature laughs in spring,
restore laughter to our lives.
When we become complaining and sour-faced,
put something funny into our minds.
Help us not to take ourselves too seriously
and to enjoy the world with you.

Restore to us, O Christ,
your rhythms that we have lost:
the rhythm of rising and sleeping;
the rhythm of rest and work;
the rhythm of breathing and walking;
the rhythm of quiet and speech;
the rhythm of loving and losing;
the rhythm of light and dark.

Christ, make us fit for purpose,
alive in heart and limb.
Christ, stretch our creaking bodies
till they tingle and feel trim.

Put fiber in our being,
take flabbiness away.
Strengthen what is weak,
keep binge and bulge at bay.

May each body be a temple
of your Spirit who is true;
a picture frame on earth
of eternity on view.

Grant us grace to
eat well,
think well,
and move well,
until our bodies, minds, and souls
are truly temples of your Holy Spirit.

Christ, today may the needs of our bodies
and the needs of our minds,
the practical needs of work,
and the social needs,
each be given their rightful place
and kept in balance.
May the needs for rest and fun,
study and sleep,
household order and justifiable work
all be answered.

Holy Christ, holy and mighty,
strip from me all that is false and out of place;
strengthen my roots in you;
bring me to that place
where I desire you alone.

Irresistible One,
when the world falls apart, be our Center;
when the world turns sour, be our Sweetness;
when we become weak, be our Strength.

We pray to you for the place of desecration:
  bring forth beauty from it.
We pray to you for the hard and barren place:
  bring forth generosity from it.
We pray to you
  for the greed- and guilt-laden place:
  bring forth forgiveness from it
  and let eternal life bloom.

Eternal Source of Life,
you are the core of our being.
Flow through our bodies
like a life-giving river.
Wash and transform the negative conditions
in our hearts, minds, bodies,
and circumstances
with light, love, and grace.

When I say "don't," would you say it like that,
Lord Christ?
When I say "them," would you say it like that,
Lord Christ?
When I say "I," would you,
who called yourself "I AM,"
strain and push like that, Lord Christ?
Break my brittle shell, Lord Christ,
and make me as human as you.

Five

Prayers for Peace and Justice

Source of Peace,
war is the price we pay
for the selfishness of nations:
Help us to wage endless war
against selfishness.
Peace is the fruit of constant endeavor
for the good:
Help us to struggle without ceasing
for good to triumph over evil.

All-seeing Restrainer,
bless the peace-makers
and encourage those
who are engaged in conflict resolution.
May more people emulate you
and reach out to those
who are different or defiant.

Christ, the peace of things above
and the stillness and rest of those below,
establish in your peace the five continents,
your universal Church, and all who seek you,
by whatever name.
Destroy wars and the causes of war
and disperse those who delight in terror.

Mighty Restorer, who brings back all,
with you we pray
to the four corners of the world:
Al-Salem, Shalom, Peace, Harmony—
with our neighbors, with our environment,
with ourselves, and with God

Beloved One,
We long to dwell always in your presence.
So help us to:
speak the truth from our hearts,
keep gossip from our tongues,
do nothing but good to others,
bless others in our use of money,
that we grow ever more secure in you.

Vast and Giving One,
wean us from attachment to possessions.
Forgive our nations for bingeing
on loans our children must repay.
Cure our addiction to debt.
Grant us mercy
as we reap what we have sown.
May we not create a spiritual famine where
abundance lies,
by failing to share the gift of our lives.

Noble Christ, take from us cynicism,
control, and mindless chatter.
Give to us wholeheartedness,
awareness, and compassion.
May we be a sacrament of strength
to those whose hands we hold,
as your strong-fingered hands hold us.
Strengthen our resolve,
sharpen our minds, shape our wills,
grace our lands.

Great Heart,
Who reaches out to all,
inspire our every nerve and sinew
to reach out to others with your love.
May we accept each person as yours.
May we include each person in our hearts.
May we find a way
to walk with those who stumble,
to watch with those who suffer,
and to work with those who avoid us.

Give us wise leaders, clear vision,
and an understanding of what is right.
Inspire in us true values.
May we know ourselves,
know what is good,
and know when to stop.
May we work toward a prejudice-free,
hate-free, fear-free world.
May we learn to celebrate with joy,
to let a thousand flowers bloom,
and to delight in one another's creativity.
May our foreign policy be
to earn the trust and gratitude of our neighbors.
May we honor one another,
seek the common good,
and live as fellow citizens
of your eternal kingdom.

Christ, help me
to take the time
to stand in the shoes of the other person,
to start from where they are,
to listen to what they feel,
to refrain from the too-hasty judgement
or the too-ready answer,
to smile and be gentle,
and yet not to collude with the slipshod,
but to prayerfully see a thing through.

In our pleasures,
your Kingdom come.
In our leaders,
your Kingdom come.
In our gatherings,
your Kingdom come.
On the roads,
your Kingdom come.
In each thing we do this day,
your Kingdom come.

Pardoner and Restorer,
help us to listen
to the story of those who are inflamed
without judgement and with empathy.

Help us to stay calm and learn what we can.
Help us to be clear
about what we can achieve,
not promise what we cannot deliver,
and take responsibility
for what we can deliver.
If it is possible,
help us to walk a mile in the other's shoes
and to want the best for them,
as for us.

We pray for an end to the injustices
that become breeding grounds of war.
We pray for the restoration of fellowship
and the building of integrity.
We pray for commitment
to the unending struggle against selfish ways
and violation of human dignity.
We pray for that peace
which is the full blossoming
of our life together.

Christ, the nations rage
and people around us become vengeful.
You see it all.
The kingdoms of this world
will become your Kingdom.
So help us look upon what is happening
with the calm assurance and quiet confidence
of the World Christ
and leave the rest to you.

You who order the universe,
pour your oil on the troubled waters
of our lives.
We bring to you the troubles
in our places of work,
in our relationships, in our church,
and in the world.
Calm us, and help us rest in you.

May we eagerly desire the best
for one another,
knowing that we share the same origin,
the same essence,
and that we are on a journey together
away from fragmentation
toward completion of all things in Christ.

Ground of All Being,
all peoples come from you.
May we honor one another
and seek the common good.
Unity of the World,
from you all peace, all justice flow.
May we cherish the web of life.

Christ, help us to see
each member of your body as you see them.
May we support each person in their calling.
May we honor the weak.
May we relate well
to other members of the body
as we make our contribution.

Christ of the scars of love,
into your hands we place
those who have been scarred by life:
those who have been betrayed,
those who have suffered loss
of limb or esteem.

Christ of the scars of love,
into your hands we place
unwanted babies,
neighbors defamed, lovers spurned.

Christ of the scars of love,
into your hands we place
those who are victims of violence,
sharp practice, or false accusation.

Christ of the scars of love,
bring healing and love
to each broken, hurting life.

Help us, O Christ,
to guard our words,
to overcome hostility with love,
to make peace
in love of the King of Life.

May your tender love burn inside us
and impel us on the road to seek for you
in the stranger's face;
or, sensing your absence,
introduce your presence.

We raise our hands
and bless the hungry and the poor.
We lay these hands
to tend the hurting and the sore.
We stretch out these hands
to welcome the stranger at the door.

Where times are dark,
where wrong parades as right,
where faith grows dim,
Christ, Light of the World,
meet us in our place of darkness.
Journey with us
and bring us to your new dawning.

Christ of the endless forcefield,
sow confusion in those
who would use terror as a means of change.
Stir conviction in those who can bring change
by acting justly and by the sharing of love.

May the light that shines out from your face
flood the world with goodness
and gather into one
a divided and broken humanity.

Christ, give us the statesmanship
of the humble heart,
the willingness to move out toward others.
Give us the faith to do our bit
that we may help to build
a civilization of love.

All-Forgiving One,
when I meet angry people
who carry centuries of hostility,
neglect, or mistreatment,
help me to listen to their story
without judgement or interruption;
and may they know
that they have met someone
who has deeply listened.

Light-Creator, evil cannot make its home
where you are welcomed in.
Forgive us for the places
where your light has been shut out.

Light-Giver,
fear and fault-finding have no place
where your love is invited in.
Forgive us for the places
where your love has been shut out.

Light-Conductor, loneliness has no place
where your saints are welcomed in.
Forgive us for the places
where we have shut them out.

May we see the face of Christ
in everyone we meet.
May everyone we meet
see the face of Christ in us

Today and always, may we
look upon each person we meet
with the eyes of Christ,
speak to each person we meet
with the words of Christ,
and go wherever we are led
with the peace of Christ.

All-Compassionate One,
pour out your compassion through us,
that we may be instruments to set others free:
those who walk through life
with their feet in fetters,
clobbered with unjust burdens,
captives in prisons of body or spirit.

Take our hands, dear Christ,
that your compassion
may flow through them out to others.
With these hands give tender touch
to those who are forgotten.
With these hands give warmth
to those left in the cold.
With these hands shield your messengers
from ills that would attack them.
With these hands
dispel darkness from the old.
With these hands
heal lost and suffering people.
Take our hands, dear Christ,
that your compassion
may flow through them out to others.

Merciful One,
may your compassion flow through our hands.
May they offer tender touch
to people who are deprived
of touch or tenderness.
May they offer human warmth
to people who are cold or dispirited.
May they offer practical care
to people who are weary and overworked.

Christ, Eternal Truth,
save us from complicity in the lie,
the refusal to speak out,
the acquiescence to misrepresentation.
Steel us to speak out,
to expose what is wrong,
to vanquish lies,
in the strength of the One
who was put to death by a lie
but remained undefeated.

Take from me, O Christ:
pride and prejudice,
hardness and hypocrisy,
selfishness and self-sufficiency,
that I may be vulnerable, like you.

May we look upon everyone
with the eyes of Christ:
shoppers and beggars,
politicians and Jihadists,
friends, critics,
and the next person we meet.

Search out in us, O Christ,
the seeds of disunity:
willfulness, insecurity, and ignorance.
Transform them
into service, trust, and awareness,
that unity in a common cause
may be born.

All-Merciful One,
you hold the poor closely to your heart:
forgive those of us who have enough
for closing our hearts to the poor.
Forgive those of us who have little
for closing our hearts to the rich.
Show us how all people and all places
can receive their worth;
in the name of the One
who had nowhere to lay his head.

We plead for your justice to fill all the lands
as the waters cover the sands.
We cry until our voices are sore.
We weep for the hungry and poor;
the children mistreated;
those damaged by force;
and the broken who can't finish their course.
We pray against cruelty, hatred, and pain;
against pride and greed for gain.
We pray for the homeless
and victims of war;
the strangers you call us to love at the door.

Help us to sense your presence among us,
O Christ,
in the gentle touch,
in the listening ear,
in the patient toil,
in the concern for the poor,
in the challenging of wrong,
in the brokenness of life.

You are here, Christ, in this place.
May your cross free it.
May your love woo it.
May your prayers hallow it.
May your peace still it.
May your life renew it.

May each land find its well-being in your will.
Give us that dynamic
that calls out and combines
the moral and spiritual
responsibility of individuals
for their immediate sphere of action.
We pray for an uprising of people
who give leadership free
from the bondage of fear,
sorry for the blindness of the past,
rising above ambition,
flexible to the direction of your Spirit,
reaching out with generous hearts
to neighboring peoples.

Christ of the loving heart,
may we look upon everyone with a smile
that reflects a ray
of the True and Universal Sun,
the smile of acceptance and understanding.
May we be builders of a world that is free
from prejudice,
Where everyone, however wayward,
is seen as a child of Love.

Your kingdom come, your will be done
on earth as it is in heaven.
Your kingdom come here
in honesty at work and home,
in fair treatment and fair trade,
in respect for human life,
in friendship between people
of different races and religions,
in freedom from hate, fear, and greed,
in generosity and goodness,
in mercy that knows no end.
Your kingdom come, your will be done
on earth as it is in heaven.

We pray for those
whose tasks are backbreaking,
whose bodies are mutilated,
or whose spirits are crushed.

Give us the will
to share our bread with the hungry,
give shelter to those who feel rejected,
and reach out to those in need.

Where people long for an end to injustice,
shine into their hearts.
Where people long for conflict to cease,
shine into their hearts.
Where people long to right
poor working conditions,
shine into their hearts.
Where people long to restore
the scarred places of earth,
shine into their hearts.
Where people long for dignity
in human relationships,
shine into their hearts.

Unfold to us
the meaning of your commission.
May we not be blind
to what you seek to accomplish.
Kindle in us the spirit of an apostle,
the willingness to pass on
what you have imparted to us.
Reveal to us what it means
to reach all the world,
whether near or far.
May every bit of the world we touch
be immersed in you.

Divine Restorer, aid us
in setting our affairs
in the simple beauty of creation.
May our belongings, activities,
and relationships
be ordered in a way that liberates the spirit.
May our clothes and furniture reflect
God-given features of our personalities.
May we set before you our income,
savings, and possessions,
conscious that we are your stewards,
not possessors of these things,
making them available as you require of us.

Christ of mercy,
your world is becoming a wasteland;
calm us to prepare a way for you.
May we discover and live
ways that are life-giving:
ways of integrity, respect,
and awareness of your presence in all.

Word of God, rays from you
light people of many beliefs.
May these rays lead us
to the places where we may sit
and eat and be one
with those who are different from us,
until you emerge in their clothes,
revealing a new facet
of your never-ending glory.

Six

Prayers of Comfort and Challenge

O Christ,
like the seed that falls into the ground
and yet bears fruit,
may we yet see the fruit
of eternal life on earth.

Christ, make us true like arrows.
Make us dependable like rock.
Make us deep like anchors.
Make us incorruptible like salt.

Christ,
to whom the spirits are subject:
cast off the works of encroaching darkness
and bring us all under
your serene and victorious reign.

Christ, you are the refined molten metal
of our human forge.
Purge our desires,
strengthen our resolve,
sharpen our minds,
shape our wills.

Sovereign of seas and stars,
hear us for ourselves and our forebears:
may your love never fail us,
may your friendship never desert us,
may paradise open its doors to us,
but always may your will be done.

Christ, we offer you our souls and bodies,
our thoughts and words and deeds,
our love for one another,
our past and our future.
Unite our will in your will.
May we and our children
grow together in love and peace
all the days of our life,
through the Christ, our Lord.

Silently the earth yields her fruits.
Silently we lie as the earth.
Do your work in us,
slowly, soundlessly.
This is the mystery of Being.
This is your Presence in us.

We make the sign of the Cross of Christ,
Our Christ, our Shield, our Savior,
each day, each night, in light, in dark,
our Treasure, our dear One,
our Eternal Home.

Christ, take my gaze away
from the false persona of myself
as always right.
Christ, take my gaze away
from my false projections of others
as the persons who are wrong.
Gently turn my gaze to you.
You see into the place of hurt
and weakness in me
and there allow love to be revealed.
Free me to see your beauty
in the face of another.

Silent, surrendered, at your feet
we bow before your presence.
Open to your every word
we linger, longing, waiting.

Christ be in the work and each thing we do.
Christ be in our hands
and each thing we touch.
Christ be in our minds
and each thing we think.
We pray for those who are jaded
by the pressures of work:
put color into their lives.
We pray for work places
where conditions are grim:
put color into these places.
We pray for ourselves in the heat
and burden of the day:
put color into our being.

Worker Christ, as we enter our workplace,
may we bring your presence with us.
Grace us to speak
your peace and perfect order
into its atmosphere.
Remind us to acknowledge your authority
over all that will be thought, decided,
and accomplished within it.
Give us a fresh supply of truth and beauty
on which to draw as we work.

Each of us has some work to do.
We do our work as to you, Christ.
We think our thoughts as to you.
We clean our rooms as to you, Christ.
We send messages as to you.
We shop and eat as to you, Christ.
We care for others as to you.

Christ, when we are weak,
remind us that your strength
can reach others through our weakness.
Open our eyes to notice what you notice.
Open our mouths
to speak one healing, life-giving word.

Christ, free us to enjoy
and not possess another;
free each of us to be ourselves,
as you created us to be.
Grant us the integrity
within which friendship thrives.
Restore the joy of communion to us.

Divine Light, encompass us;
penetrate our souls,
our minds, and our bodies.
Cleansing, healing Soul-Light,
shine out into our business dealings;
shine out into all human dealings;
shine out into the architecture of life.

Give to us thoughts greater
than our own thoughts,
prayers deeper than our own prayers.
Give to us the arts of prayer—
prayers that rise like incense,
and thoughts that penetrate to the Throne.

Christ, we have not much faith,
and we can't help it.
But help us to use the little faith we have,
so that it grows day by day.
May we daily increase in trust and in valor.

Christ, make our lives an open book
that good people may read.
Take from us the judging heart
and the spirit that bangs doors shut.
Weed out falseness.
Help us accept our weakness.
May our light shine.

You are the refined molten forge
of the human race.
Purge us of all that is false and unreal;
forge our characters until we are true:
true to ourselves, to others, to you.

In the flavor of a fruit,
in the flowing of a stream,
in the feeling of a sunset,
may we know that you are good.

Make us attentive to the lap of the waves.
Make us attentive to
the movements of the sky.
Make us attentive to the grasses that grow.
Make us attentive to the soul's every sigh.
Make us aware of the landscape that passes.
Make us aware of new scapes coming in.
Make us aware of your precious heartbeats.
Make us aware of the world within.

Christ, you are our island;
in your bosom we rest.
You are the calm of the sea;
in that peace we stay.
You are the deep waves of the shining ocean;
with their eternal sound we sing.
You are the song of the birds;
in that tune is our joy.
You are the smooth white sand of the shore;
in you is no gloom.
You are the breaking
of the waves on the rock;
your praise is echoed in the swell.
You are the Lover of our lives;
in you we dwell.

Uncreated Beauty,
who graces everything that has been created,
as the hand is made for holding
and the eyes for seeing,
grant that we may behold your beauty
in the lovers' embrace,
in a mother's love,
in the face of a steadfast father,
in the life of the valiant woman
and the gentle man,
and in the twilight of the gloaming;
until the beauty that is within us
comes forth and sings to you.

May the Sun of suns shine upon us,
bringing peace and poise.
May the healing rays come through us
until we frolic like the lambs.

Gracious Christ,
may your glory be seen
in the stature of waiting.
May your glory be seen
in the grace of unknowing.
May your glory be seen
in the dignity of humbling.

Give us the eye of the eagle that
gazes into your face,
traces the movements of your hand,
penetrates the depths of your heart,
scans the reaches of your mind,
and glimpses the horizons of your Spirit.

In your presence
we affirm that every organ,
action, and function of our bodies
is animated by your living Spirit.
By day and by night
may your Life flowing through us
renew every cell of our bodies
after your indwelling image.

Make us rich in your eyes, dear Christ.
Help us to take freely
of the treasures of heaven.
Clothe us in the virtues
whose attractions increase.
Feed us with food that never goes bad.
Adorn us with beauty that never fades.
Free us to stride through
the courts of mammon,
uncluttered by its enticements,
content with you.

Divine Artist,
the world is your canvas,
and we your prime exhibits.
Bring to flower the artist
you have planted within us
and transform art to become
a panorama of healing.

Come like fire and warm our hearts.
Come like wind and refresh our frames.
Come like water and revive our souls.
Come like the earth and nourish our being.

Help me conquer anger by gentleness,
greed by generosity.
apathy by fervor.

Immerse us in your pure water
and your gift of your tender heart.
Immerse us in your healing water
and your gift of wisdom.
Immerse us in your renewing waters
and your gift of reverence.

You are the well of heaven.
When we visit wells of the earth,
the way to you is opened.
Touch us. Refresh us. Heal us.
Flow over us and make us whole.

Light-Bringer,
we have buried your insight
beneath falsehoods.
We have insulated ourselves
from being vulnerable to others.
We have been closed
to your renewing of our mind.
Break through our resistance.
Free us from the past.
Open our hearts to love.

You are the Vine.
We are the branches.
Everything we need in life
we find in you, our Source.
What has died, we'll pass it by.
When you prune, we will let go.
Live in us, Christ,
and we will live in you.

Christ, we leave behind with you
affections, habits, and attitudes
that are no part of a whole life.
This one thing we do:
we look to you and to the fellowship
of your sufferings
and to the power of your resurrection
and to the goal of the whole created universe
becoming one with you.
So help us God.

Make us
patient in our observing,
sensitive in our listening,
generous in our befriending,
and compelling in our speaking,
that we may open new frontiers for you.

O Holy Fire,
O Holy Grace,
O Overflowing Silent One:
by your birth
enable us;
by your overcoming of spirits
arm us;
by your integrity
make us true;
by your fortitude in trials
establish us;
by your self-giving in death
change us;
by your mission to unquiet spirits
raise us.

Eternal Mind, thank you for our minds
that make sense of the world.
Eternal Beauty, thank you for the beauty
that puts soul into the world.
Eternal Life, thank you for the lives
that point beyond themselves.

Help us, Christ,
to trade with the gifts you have given us
and to bend our minds to holy learning,
that we may escape the fretting moth
of littleness of mind
that would wear out our souls.
Brace our wills to actions
that they may not be the spoils
of weak desires.
Train our hearts and lips
to song which gives courage to the soul.
Being buffeted by trials,
may we learn to laugh.
Being reproved, may we give thanks.
Having failed,
may we determine to succeed.

Christ, Lord of Order and Beauty,
help us to clothe our bodies and our homes
with beauty appropriate to the season.
Give to us a sense of balance and of order,
with room for spontaneity.
Show us what bubbles and what brings calm,
what brings energy and what brings charm.

Christ of fearless love,
take us to our point of greatest weakness
and let us find you there.
May your strength
be made complete in our frailty.

As fish live in water may we live in you.
As birds soar high and carefree
may we soar with you.
As deer run straight and graceful
may we run with you.
As water flows so freely
may we flow with you.

Gentle Christ, reveal to us
the beauty of sensitive friendship.
Help us to create such stillness
in our inner being
that we become aware
of your gracious movements
in the souls of others.

Thank you for the gift of a good soul friend:
a companion on a long journey,
a fire for a cold hearth,
an anchor to a ship adrift,
a pruning knife to an overgrown plant,
a window onto a new world
gentle rain on new seeds.
Thank you for the gift of a soul friend.

Into your hands, O Christ,
we release the work we shall leave behind,
the pressures that weary us,
the problems that would pursue us,
the things we have neglected,
the tasks left unfinished.

We are sorry for the distractions
that turn our thoughts away from you
to selfish pursuits.
Help us to recover a sense of belonging
by returning to the Ground
from which we all come.

Eternal Now,
you enter into time:
you guided Moses' people
through the Red Sea;
you were born of Mary in a cow shed;
you will be present
when the cosmos comes to its end.
Eternal Now, you are beyond time,
you are Presence.

Eternal Now, your second coming is surely
not after the first and before a third—
Could it be our coming
into the Eternal Presence?
Help me to become present.

May my human nature become one with you
as two pieces of wax become one
when they are melted together.
I pray for this second coming
within my own life.

May the fire of the Christ-Spirit
kindle in us a great blaze,
consuming all that is false,
leaving only that which is God.

About the Author

RAY SIMPSON is a founding guardian of the international Community of Aidan and Hilda. In 2016 he moved from the Holy Island of Lindisfarne, UK, where the Community has a base for resources, study, and retreat, to a new Community House in Berwick-Upon-Tweed on the nearby mainland. Ray is the author of numerous bestselling books on Celtic spirituality, including *The Celtic Book of Days: Wisdom from the Ancient Saints for Each Day of the Year* and *Celtic Christianity: Deep Roots for a Modern Faith.*

Celtic Christianity
Deep Roots for a Modern Faith

Celtic Spirituality for the Modern World

The world of the long-ago Celts appeals to many of us in the twenty-first century. Whether we are looking to find our cultural heritage or are seeking an alternative to worn and restrictive religious forms, the earth-centered, woman-friendly, inclusive faith of the Christian Celts offers us a deep-rooted alternative approach to traditional Christianity. Theirs was a church without walls, which lived naturally and comfortably

within the community. Ray Simpson has spent most of his life walking in the footsteps of the Christian Celts, and now he allows us to experience for ourselves their dynamic spirituality.

Paperback Price: $24.95

Kindle Price: $8.99

Celtic Book of Days
Ancient Wisdom for Each Day of the Year from the Celtic Followers of Christ

The ancient Celts found God's presence in each ordinary moment of the day. Everything they encountered revealed to them the presence of the sacred; each day was deep with meaning. Now you too can practice the Celts' faith, as you take a few moments to immerse yourself in their wisdom. These small daily moments of reflection and insight will open your heart to each day and all it holds.

Paperback Price: $28.99

Kindle Price: $9.99

Earth Afire with God
Celtic Prayers for Ordinary Life

Here are prayers and blessings that sanctify the simplest of daily activities. They remind us to look for the holiness of the everyday and the real presence of God in Creation. They will illumine your life.

Paperback Price: $12.95

Kindle Price: $3.99

Water from an Ancient Well
Celtic Spirituality for Modern Life

A Fresh Look at Celtic Spirituality

Using story, scripture, reflection, and prayer, this book offers readers a taste of the living water that refreshed the ancient Celts. The author invites readers to imitate the Celtic saints who were aware of God as a living presence in everybody and everything. This ancient perspective gives radical new alternatives to modern faith practices, ones that are both challenging and constructively positive. This is a Christianity big enough to embrace the entire world.

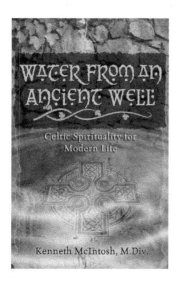

Paperback Price: $19.99

Kindle Price: $7.49

ANAMCHARA
BOOKS

AnamcharaBooks.com

CPSIA information can be obtained
at www.ICGtesting.com
Printed in the USA
BVHW031306090421
604608BV00005B/98